THE DYING SEA

© Aladdin Books Ltd 1992

*First published in the
United States in 1992 by*
Gloucester Press
95 Madison Avenue
New York, NY 10016

ISBN 0-531-17385-2

Library of Congress Catalog
Card Number 88-50523

Printed in Belgium

The original edition of this title was published in the **Survival** series.

The front cover shows a striped dolphin caught up in a drift net from a French fishing boat.

Contents

THE DYING SEA

Michael Bright

Gloucester Press

New York : London : Toronto : Sydney

Introduction

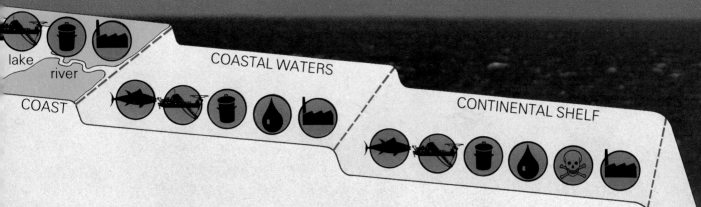

lake river COAST COASTAL WATERS CONTINENTAL SHELF

The sea is the engine room of the planet. It influences the world's weather patterns and maintains the balance of gases in the atmosphere. It also provides the water – via the clouds and rain – which is needed by life on land. But the sea is vulnerable to upset and abuse. And if the sea is upset, all of life on Earth can be upset.

The sea covers seven-tenths of the world's surface. There are big seas – the Atlantic, Pacific and Indian Oceans – which are deeper than the highest mountains are tall. There are small seas, like the Caribbean and the Red Sea, which have formed as a result of major movements of the Earth's crust. There are seas with no tides, like the Mediterranean, and there are inland seas, such as the Caspian and the Great Lakes.

Lakes and rivers run into the sea, taking excess water and garbage from the land. Society uses the sea directly as a dumping ground. Every day millions of tons of refuse are thrown into the sea – some of which will never break down. We also use the sea for food, transport, fuel supplies and building materials. But these activities interfere with natural cycles. Millions of different sea creatures live in particular conditions in the sea and they are linked together in a delicate balance of food chains. Our activities destroy life in the oceans. Unless they are controlled, they will ultimately threaten our own survival.

The diagram shows how society uses and abuses the sea, whether it is in the coastal waters or in the deepest of the deeps. Because the sea is used for so many different purposes, some activities conflict seriously with others. For example, the dumping of chemical wastes into the sea is not compatible with safe fishing.

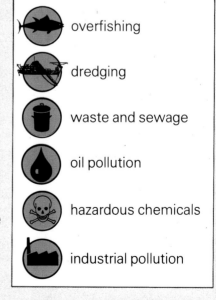

overfishing

dredging

waste and sewage

oil pollution

hazardous chemicals

industrial pollution

THE DEEP TRENCH

Currents and chemicals

People once thought that waste materials poured into the sea would be diluted and would disappear forever. But materials are always on the move in the sea. Currents move wastes from one place to another, concentrating them here and diluting them there. Upwellings, areas where colder water from the depths is brought to the surface, can even unearth dangerous wastes buried where they were thought to be safe.

Sea creatures do not choose between safe food and food contaminated with dangerous wastes. They eat both. Once chemicals have entered the food chain, they are concentrated as they move further up the chain. The pesticides DDT and dieldrin were banned from agricultural use many years ago and were thought to have disappeared. The levels of DDT and dieldrin found in sparrow hawks that hunt inland have decreased since the ban. But the levels in the tissues of birds hunting by the sea are actually increasing. The chemicals were washed from the land to the sea via rivers ("runoff"). Over many years they built up in marine food chains. They are now at dangerous levels in the top predators – animals like birds of prey and humans.

▷ The white-bellied sea eagle, seen here catching a fish, lives between India, China and northern Australia. In this area, pesticides harmful to birds of prey are still being used. As a result, the eggs of many species are likely to suffer eggshell thinning. Bird populations will decline – just as they did in North America and Europe in the 1960s.

The body of a golden eagle, found dying on the Scottish island of Lewis in 1987, was analyzed for dangerous chemicals. It contained the highest levels of DDT and dieldrin ever found in a bird of prey. It had been catching and eating birds, which in turn had been eating fish which contained these chemicals.

▽ This diagram shows what happens to a chemical that is sprayed on the land.

Rain washes the chemicals from the soil into streams, rivers and finally the sea.

Phytoplankton (plant-like microorganisms) take up the chemicals.

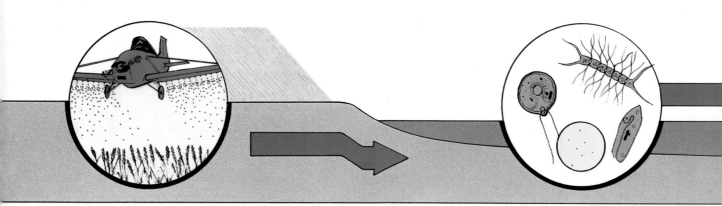

"We dump pollutants seemingly out of sight in the rivers and sea, but they eventually come back to us on our dinner tables - in the fish and shellfish that we eat."

Jacques-Yves Cousteau, underwater explorer and pioneer

Zooplankton (minute animals) eat phytoplankton and so concentrate the chemicals.

Small fish eat the zooplankton and larger fish eat the small fish.

Chemicals become more concentrated and are finally eaten by top predators.

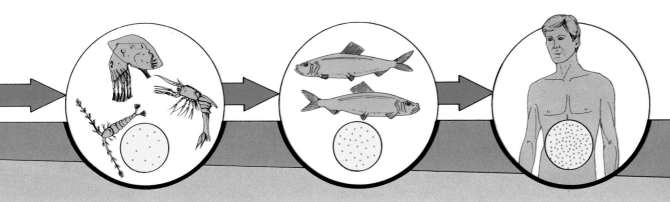

Overfishing

The oceans were once thought to be filled with limitless stocks of fish, whales and seals. But this is far from the truth. North Sea herrings, Peruvian anchovies, Northeast Atlantic basking sharks and Namibian pilchards are just some of the fisheries which have disappeared, probably because of overfishing. In the past every whale population in the world was brought, one at a time, to the edge of extinction. But despite these warnings, stocks of fish are still being removed from the oceans.

We know little about the biology of many sea creatures or how many there are, yet more and more sophisticated methods are being used to catch them. Today fish factory ships and fleets of catcher boats are used to catch as many fish as they can in the shortest possible time.

In 1983 the UN Food and Agriculture Organization noted that 11 major oceanic fisheries were near collapse. Fisheries account for 23% of the world's protein. To lose about 11 million tons of fish each year is serious for the poorer nations that depend on the sea for food.

▽ The fish in this photograph are being loaded onto Soviet factory ships known as "klondikers" — named after the mining district in North America. It is a reminder that fish are still "mined," like coal, with little regard for good management.

Nobody knows what impact overfishing really has on the species being fished, or on the other creatures that depend on them for food. But we know that intense fishing upsets the balance of life in the oceans. In the Antarctic huge quantities of krill and squid are removed every year. Many people are concerned that if these marine stocks are reduced, it will have a serious effect on the seals, seabirds, penguins and baleen whales that feed on them.

△ These shark fins drying in the sun in the Middle East are destined for soup in Japan. The rest of the shark is wastefully thrown away. Sharks tend to live in specific areas and are slow to breed. If a local shark population is fished out, there is a chance it will not recover.

9

Dredging

There are valuable materials at the bottom of the sea. As with overfishing, they are often removed without much thought to the effect this has on the marine environment. Bucket and suction dredgers work coastal waters and estuaries to obtain sand and gravel to build highways and other projects. Most of them work in areas where it is supposed that they do least damage. But some will dredge anywhere, and this can have serious consequences.

Dredgers may remove sand banks that protect shorelines from the force of the sea. This can result in serious damage to the coastline and the destruction of salt marshes and other habitats important to wildlife. Dredging can also destroy the spawning sites of fish which live on the seabed and it removes the plants and animals living there. It can turn the sea bottom into a vast underwater desert.

Shipping channels often silt up and have to be dredged. The dredged material is dumped elsewhere in the sea, causing the water to become muddy. Light cannot penetrate and this has disastrous effects on marine life.

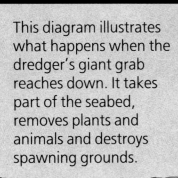

This diagram illustrates what happens when the dredger's giant grab reaches down. It takes part of the seabed, removes plants and animals and destroys spawning grounds.

sandbanks removed causing coastal erosion

plant and animal life uprooted

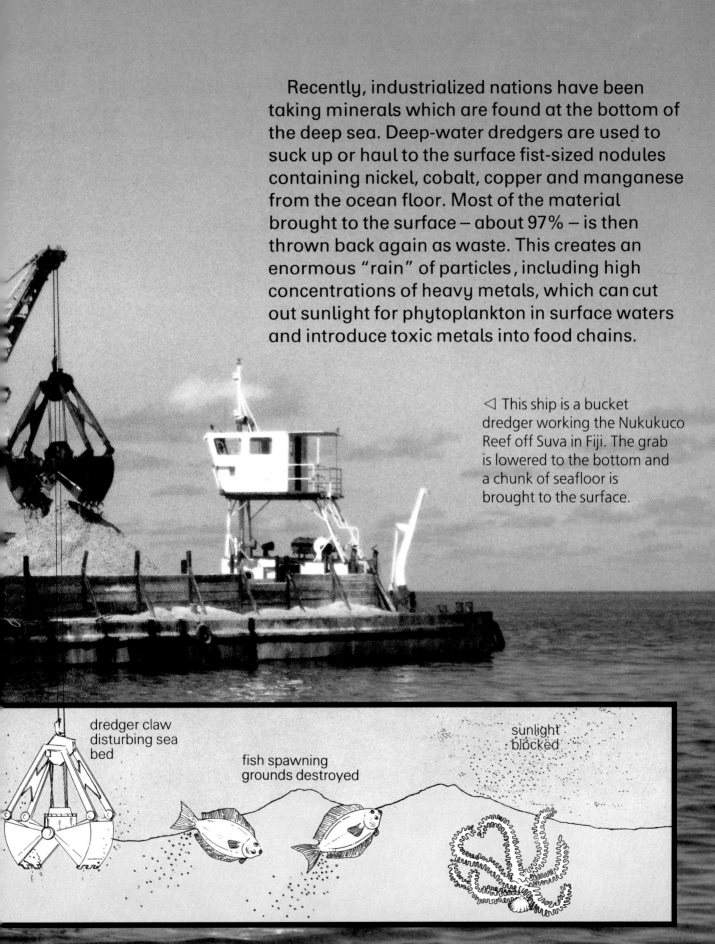

Recently, industrialized nations have been taking minerals which are found at the bottom of the deep sea. Deep-water dredgers are used to suck up or haul to the surface fist-sized nodules containing nickel, cobalt, copper and manganese from the ocean floor. Most of the material brought to the surface – about 97% – is then thrown back again as waste. This creates an enormous "rain" of particles, including high concentrations of heavy metals, which can cut out sunlight for phytoplankton in surface waters and introduce toxic metals into food chains.

◁ This ship is a bucket dredger working the Nukukuco Reef off Suva in Fiji. The grab is lowered to the bottom and a chunk of seafloor is brought to the surface.

dredger claw disturbing sea bed

fish spawning grounds destroyed

sunlight blocked

The coral reefs

A coral reef is a vast living community. It is mainly composed of lime laid down by millions of coral polyps, tiny animals like sea anemones. It is a haven for marine wildlife and has more sea creatures than many other areas of the sea. The rich diversity of marine life provides much needed food, attracts tourists and in some parts of the world, the coral reef is important to a country's economy. There is therefore good reason to keep reefs in a healthy condition. But there are problems. The polyps, and the algae that live in their tissues and help in their growth, can be damaged by pollution, diseases, predators and changes in seawater and light conditions. Human activities are upsetting conditions on the reefs.

The Crown-of-Thorns Starfish

The Crown-of-Thorns Starfish is a large, spiny starfish about the size of a dinner plate. It lives in tropical water and feeds on coral. It eats by inverting its stomach over the coral and digests the polyps where they are. Unlike the coral it is unaffected by pollution. Scientists are trying to control starfish by injecting each one with a poison.

In Australia, the Great Barrier Reef is threatened by the Crown-of-Thorns Starfish. Thousands of these starfishes are feeding on the coral polyps and are consequently destroying the reef. The reason for their population explosion is not known. Collection of triton shells (the starfish's main predator) and the catching of fish that feed on starfish eggs are possible causes of the destruction of the world's largest reef.

▽ Coral reefs in Bali not only attract visitors, they also provide raw materials for the lime industry. Sadly, it was not realized that the reefs were protecting the island shoreline until it was too late. Removal of large portions of reef have resulted in the serious coastal damage seen below.

Coral polyps prefer warm, clear conditions. Reefs in waters close to mining operations, such as the reef in Kenya in the inset, are smothered by waste silt and die. The coral is killed and the reef is deserted by all other living things.

In the world's tropical seas coral reefs are being destroyed. Topsoil is washed into the sea after vegetation is removed to make way for crops or tourist buildings. The soil causes the reef to silt up. Sewage from towns and fertilizers from farms cause algae to bloom which use up all the oxygen in the water, killing the coral polyps. Industrial pollution kills all reef life, and the trade in corals is helping to destroy enormous sections of the reefs. Oil pollution poisons coral polyps and waste materials from mining, such as bauxite works in the Caribbean islands, choke the reefs. Damaged reefs no longer grow and they cannot provide suitable places for fish and other marine creatures to live and breed.

The marine dump

For centuries, the sea has been the place where much of humankind's wastes have been dumped. Ships' crews, for example, traditionally threw their garbage over the side. Coastal towns discharged their raw sewage into the sea. In the past, the amount of garbage was comparatively small and was quickly broken down by the sea. Today, the amount of wastes are much greater and the materials are also more permanent. The oceans are becoming choked.

△ South American sea lion with packing strap

"It is now routine to see man-made debris floating on the ocean surface far from land - a condition that did not exist a few years ago."

Dr James Heirtzler, NASA, Goddard Space Flight Center

△ Pacific fur seal with fishing net

△ Californian sea lion with yoke from beverage cans

△ These photographs show how litter causes suffering for marine wildlife. Plastic straps choke animals or cut into their flesh as they grow. Wounds become infected and the animals die slowly.

Plastics pollution facts
● 26,000 tons of plastic packaging are dumped at sea each year
● 690,000 plastic containers are dumped by the world's ships every day
● 3,000 miles of nylon drift nets are set each night
● 6 miles of fishing net are lost each night

◁ This photograph shows the garbage washed up on Venice Beach in California.

Society's garbage has created a plague for marine life. Plastic bags mistaken for jellyfish are eaten by sea turtles and whales. The animals choke and die. A sperm whale was once found with 50 plastic bags stuck in its throat. Seabirds eat tiny styrofoam balls that float on the sea's surface. They make the birds feel as if they are full and so prevent them from eating proper food. They do not put on fat and so their fitness for survival in the wild is reduced.

In the Aleutian Islands of the North Pacific the fur seal population has gone down by nearly 10%, not from hunting or a decrease in fish stocks, but because they get trapped in plastic packing straps and the plastic yokes that hold beverage containers together. A million miles of nylon fishing nets, known as the curtain of death, are set annually. And more than 600 miles are lost each year. These "ghost nets" continue to fish uncontrolled. They catch and drown sea turtles, seals, seabirds, dolphins and whales. At the end of 1988 an international treaty will come into force that makes it illegal to dump plastics or nylon nets at sea.

Oil pollution

Oil pollution at sea poses a great threat to wildlife. The oil comes from a variety of sources. There are natural seepages, discharges of fuel oil from ships, spillages from oil refineries and oil platforms, tanker accidents and the residues from cleaning out the tanks of tankers. But by far the greatest source is in the run-off from rivers that have banks lined with industries.

Oil pollution takes the form of oil slicks, oil globules, and recently, plasto-tar balls. These are balls of tar surrounded by plastic garbage. Normally, oil breaks down very slowly into less harmful substances, but because of the plastic, these tar balls will drift around the oceans for decades to come.

▽ The photograph below shows an oil platform and pipeline damaged during the Gulf War in 1991. Iraqi leader Saddam Hussein is thought to have deliberately released oil into the sea. In just 10 minutes, one ton of oil can spread 150 feet across the sea's surface to a thickness of 4 in. Oil pollution can cause the deaths of seabirds, fish and also sea mammals like seals and otters.

"We cannot expect that problems of pollutants we have only just discovered will be solved at the stroke of a pen."

Marine Pollution Bulletin

International agreements have meant that oil pollution in the world's oceans has been reduced in recent years. The focus of future concern, however, is in the polar regions. Oil is being extracted from under the Arctic Ocean. Oil globules from accidental spillages get frozen into the ice when the sea freezes. The oil is black and absorbs heat. This causes the ice to melt once more. If there were a serious spillage, large areas of pack ice would turn to seawater. This, in turn, would influence the local climate, which would have effects on other regions. Life at sea and on land could be seriously disturbed.

The Dugong

Dugongs, or sea cows, were once mistaken for mermaids. They stand upright in the water and the females appear to cradle their young. They live along the shores of East Africa, Southeast Asia and around northern Australia.

◁ Over the last decade, the wars in the Persian Gulf have included attacks on many oil facilities. Dugongs have suffered badly from the resulting oil slicks. The Gulf's dugong population is now perilously low.

SURVIVAL PROFILE...

Life at the surface

Life at the surface of the sea, such as plankton and seabirds, is most likely to suffer the consequences of oil pollution. Every year many millions of birds, such as penguins, divers, cormorants and sea ducks, are killed because they dive to avoid hazards and to catch food. Seabirds passing in a storm will often mistake an oil slick for a patch of calm water – oil can flatten a rough sea – and swoop down to rest. They become trapped in the black sticky mess. By attempting to preen their feathers, some birds eat the oil and eventually die from liver and kidney failure. Oil clogs up their feathers, affecting buoyancy and insulation. This causes many birds to die of exposure.

▽ Puffins are vulnerable to oil on the surface of the sea. Slicks that drift into feeding areas and close to breeding colonies have the greatest impact. The long-term effect on bird populations is not clear. But where large spills have taken place, such as in the English Channel where the *Torrey Canyon* and the *Amoco Cadiz* accidents devastated vast stretches of coastline, puffin numbers have declined dramatically.

The Puffin
Puffins are accomplished divers. They catch fish under the sea and bring them back to the breeding colony in their bills. They breed in burrows which they either excavate themselves or they take over abandoned rabbit burrows.

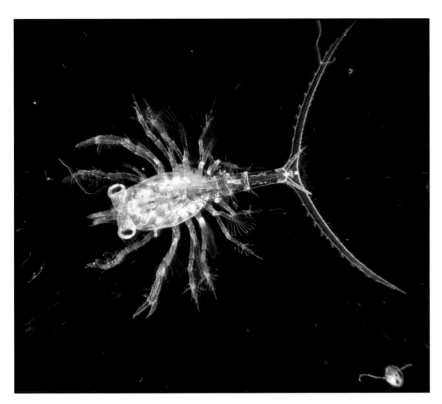

Plankton

Microscopic plants and animals, known as plankton, drift in the top layers of the sea. Phytoplankton (plants) use energy from the sun to convert carbon and water into billions of tons of living tissue – the basic food for all life in the sea.

◁ This tiny larva of a lobster is one of the creatures which make up zooplankton – the drifting animal life that eats the phytoplankton. There are signs that oil pollution can cause malformations in developing fish eggs and marine larvae.

▷ This photograph shows a colony of guillemots on the Stack Rock in the Farne Islands off the northeast coast of England. A huge number of birds, gathering at a single breeding site, is vulnerable to an oil spill incident. An entire population could be wiped out overnight. It is seabirds like these that are good indicators of the state of our environment – if only we had the good sense to watch them. Seabirds were the first to reveal the extent to which pesticides had become widely distributed through the seas. When tens of thousands of birds wash ashore it indicates oil pollution. Starving seabirds and deserted colonies warn us when a fishery is about to collapse.

The Guillemot

This bird spends most of its time at sea, only returning to the cliffs to breed. It is found around all the coasts bordering the North Atlantic and Pacific Oceans.

Hazardous chemicals

In recent years, some of the most dangerous substances ever known have been created, such as radioactive plutonium and highly poisonous chemicals called dioxins. But what happens to these substances when they are not needed any more? Often the answer has been to pack them into drums and dump them into the sea. Many people are concerned that the drums will corrode and the materials leak out. If this were to happen, they would enter the food chains and turn up once more, just like the pesticides.

New ways are constantly being sought for the disposal of hazardous materials. One method is to burn chemicals on incinerator ships at sea at a temperature of 2,200°F. This turns most of the materials into relatively safe substances.

◁ In the photograph, canisters of nuclear waste are being dumped from *The Gem* into the Atlantic.

But scientists are concerned about the 0.01% (one ton in 10,000) of toxic waste not destroyed by burning. They fear that when the smoke settles on the water downwind of the ship, hazardous materials could enter the sea and get into the food chain. For this reason, the International Maritime Organization has now banned ocean incineration in the North Sea. Another plan to dispose of dangerous waste involves dumping it into the deepest parts of the ocean. In the future, sewage sludge, industrial waste and toxic ash from incinerator plants may be dropped to the abyssal plain, three miles down. Scientists claim that if the area is monitored, the vast amount of ocean water should safely dilute the contaminants.

"Over an extended period of time the introduction of pollutants into the oceans could lead to a long-term build-up of toxic material, causing widespread mortalities and morbidities in ocean organisms. Once this condition is reached there is no turning back."

Professor Edward Goldberg,
Scripps Institution of Oceanography

◁ Drums containing dangerous chemicals do not always stay in the deep sea where they were dumped or where they washed overboard in an accident. Some are swept up in ocean currents and are carried to beaches. If the drums are damaged by waves or rocks, the contents might leak out and cause danger to people and wildlife.

One hazardous chemical that has been introduced into the marine environment is an anti-fouling paint called tributyltin (or TBT). This is painted on ships' bottoms to keep them free of barnacles and weeds. TBT contains the metal tin, and when the paint slowly leaks into the sea the tin has a serious effect on wildlife. An amount the size of an aspirin is sufficient to kill all the marine organisms nearby. Oysters, for example, have suffered from TBT poisoning.

The Mediterranean

The Mediterranean Sea has all the problems associated with society's abuse of the marine environment. It is a semienclosed sea which is virtually tideless and it loses more water through evaporation than from outflow. The water mass is exchanged with the Atlantic every 70 years. So anything that is poured into the Mediterranean stays there. All major sources of pollution can be found around its shores. Over 100 million people live there and the sea has the highest concentration of ships in the world. The main problems are raw sewage from towns and cities, particularly from tourist resorts, the discharge of heavy metals from industries and the disturbance of wildlife by tourism.

◁ These large fish are tuna, an important harvest in Sicily. But they are being contaminated by high levels of heavy metals, including mercury, lead, cadmium, and titanium, from industries and natural sources.

In 1972, the Mediterranean was considered the most badly polluted sea in the world. In the Northern Adriatic off Venice and Trieste large areas of the sea bottom were completely empty of life. Something had to be done. So in 1980 some of the nations that border the sea signed a treaty to clean it up. Before the action, 33% of beaches were so polluted that they were declared unfit for bathing. Today all except five have passed their health tests. New sewage plants are being built in many cities, and industries are no longer able to dump wastes which contain certain chemicals. However, nothing is being done to limit the disturbance of wildlife in coastal waters by tourist traffic.

▷ This pipe is discharging raw sewage into the sea. Sewage provides high levels of nutrients for marine plants which use up all the oxygen and so the animals die.

◁ Around the southern end of Italy, heavy metal pollution is not entirely the result of industrial discharges. Mt Etna, seen erupting in 1985, ejects vast quantities of ash and dust.

23

SURVIVAL PROFILE...

At the brink of extinction

Many animals that live in, or obtain their food from the sea, have been hit hard by pollution, overfishing and human disturbance. Seals, birds of prey and sea turtles are among the worst affected. A few, like the monk seals, have been brought close to extinction or, in the case of the Caribbean monk seal, have already died out. The plight of others, like the white-tailed sea eagle, has been noticed – but only just in time. They, like sea turtles, are still in danger.

> **The Monk Seal**
> These seals live in tropical waters. There are two surviving species – the Hawaiian and Mediterranean monk seals. They are the most primitive of seals. The last reliable sighting of the Caribbean species was in 1952.

△ This Hawaiian monk seal is found to breed on just six atolls in the Pacific. There are thought to be no more than 500 left.

The Mediterranean monk seal breeds in caves, often near to vacation beaches. Disturbance causes mother seals to abort fetuses and abandon pups.

There are plans in Hawaii and in the Mediterranean to protect the seals by creating "no-go" areas to keep noisy tourists away from seals.

The Loggerhead Turtle
This large sea turtle lives on shellfish, jellyfish, sponges and fish. It is found throughout the warm seas of the world. Only females come onto land to lay and bury their eggs on sandy beaches. Their eggs are eaten by coastal peoples.

◁ This female loggerhead has just completed egg-laying on a sandy beach. In the future she may find her egg-laying site destroyed or disturbed. Turtle beaches are under threat from tourist developments.

▽ The white-tailed sea eagles in Rhum, Scotland are a success story. The eagles were brought to Rhum from Scandinavia, where a special diet of pesticide-free food enabled wild populations to increase once more and return from the brink of extinction.

White-tailed Sea Eagle
This eagle has an enormous wing span and a broad wedge-shaped white tail in adults. It once thrived throughout northern Europe. DDT and eggshell thinning reduced numbers to such an extent that only a handful survive on the shores of the Baltic Sea.

The Great Lakes

The Great Lakes of North America, a collection of inland freshwater "seas," make up the largest natural reservoir of freshwater in the world. The St Lawrence River and the canals of the accompanying Seaway connect the lakes to the Atlantic Ocean. The shores are lined with industry, chemical works, oil installations and docks.

A few years ago, pollution levels became so serious that aquatic life developed abnormally. Cancerous growths appeared on fish and sections of the southern lakes were totally dead. The numbers of native fish species, such as lake herring and sturgeon, declined. Lake trout populations were devastated by sea lampreys that entered the Lakes when the Seaway was opened. The blue pike became extinct.

Measures are now being taken to stop raw sewage, chemical pollution and agricultural run-off from entering the lake system. There is also a program to redevelop fisheries. But it will take a long time for the Lakes to recover from the many years of neglect.

▽ The steel works in this photograph is at Hamilton on Lake Ontario. It uses the lake for cooling water, effluent disposal, and for transporting material to and from the plant. It is one of many steel works built on the shores of the Great Lakes supplying steel for the automobile industry.

CANADA

Lake Superior

Lake Huron

Lake Ontario

USA

Lake Michigan

Lake Erie

▷ The beluga or white whale is an animal of the Arctic. Some groups feed and breed in the St Lawrence estuary. Here they are vulnerable to disturbance by shipping and whale-watching tourists, loss of food stocks because of hydroelectric dams, and pollution from industry. Some belugas from this estuary have become so contaminated with toxic chemicals that they cannot breed and will die out.

▽ The St Lawrence Seaway and the Great Lakes system allows large ocean-going ships to penetrate 2,340 miles into the heart of the North American continent. The cost of building the Seaway was $470 million. The cost to the environment is incalculable

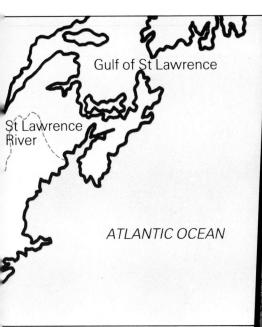

Gulf of St Lawrence

St Lawrence River

ATLANTIC OCEAN

A future for the sea

◁ This photograph shows conservationists attempting to block a toxic waste outfall. Conservation pressure groups like Greenpeace use such actions to draw public and government attention to environmental abuse. Some governments, mainly those from the wealthy industrial nations, are in a position to right their wrongs. The less wealthy are less likely to act.

Since humankind first set foot in the sea it has muddied the waters. But recent years of environmental upsets has made us realize that the oceans are not so vast and they are not a limitless natural resource that can be exploited without check. Today, the world is concerned about the state of the seas.

The United Nations' regional seas programs monitor problem areas, draw plans for action and bring together the international community to put things right. There are several international treaties. The London Dumping Convention has banned the dumping of heavy metal and cancer producing wastes in the world's seas, and the Oslo Treaty has blacklisted chemicals that cannot be discharged into the North Sea and North-east Atlantic. The Convention on the Conservation of Antarctic Marine Living Resources concerns itself with the fragile ecosystem in the Southern Ocean.

The condition of some of the most polluted seas, like the Baltic and the Mediterranean, is already beginning to improve. There is, it seems, the international will to look after the world's seas. The seas *can* continue to live, and if there is any future for life on earth, the seas *must* live.

◁ Here Greenpeace divers in the Irish Sea are trying to block a nuclear waste discharge pipe from the nuclear reprocessing plant at Sellafield in England. They received a three-month prison sentence for this action and Greenpeace made an out-of-court settlement of $140,000 in damages.

Hard facts

Arabian Sea
High levels of DDT were detected for the first time during 1987 in zooplankton samples taken from the eastern part of the sea. Huge quantities of pesticides used for agriculture (India alone spreads 55,000 tons each year on its land) are clearly beginning to find their way into marine food chains.

Australasia
Beaches in Australia and New Zealand have become the trash cans of the Southern Hemisphere. Any garbage thrown into the water at the southern end of the world enters ocean currents and eventually ends up on Australian beaches.

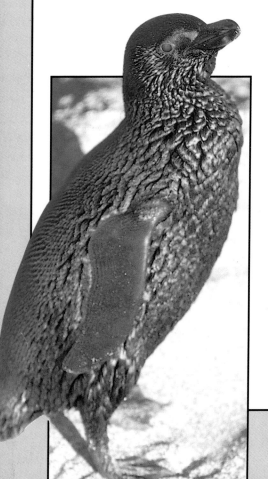

Baltic Sea
Gray seals have been found in this tideless sea with hideous deformations on their lower jaws and flippers. Liver cancers and breakdowns of the seals' immune systems (similar to the human disease AIDS) have also been detected.

Caribbean Sea and the Gulf of Mexico
Pesticide run-off from the large number of farms in this region is the greatest threat to these waters. The Mississippi River system carries agricultural run-off from 41% of the land surface of the United States. South and Central American countries are still using dangerous pesticides banned in the U.S. Fertilizers cause algae to bloom, which then remove oxygen from the water. A section of the sea off the Louisiana coast has been declared dead. Fertilizer run-off carried by the Mississippi River is blamed.

North Sea
Sewage dumped from barges and discharged from pipes, heavy metals washed in from industrialized rivers, nuclear wastes from reprocessing plants and power stations, and organic chemicals such as DDT from river run-off makes the North Sea one of the most polluted in the world. Diseased seals and malformed bottom-dwelling fish may be warning of environmental disaster. A German survey of fish catches in the North Sea in 1991 discovered that many fish are suffering from tumors, bacterial ulcers and liver damage. One third of the fish caught at the mouth of the River Tay on the east coast of Scotland had tumors.

Pacific Ocean
In October 1991, the Surfriding Foundation of Los Angeles successfully sued two papermills that had polluted the sea in northern California. The two companies had exceeded pollution limits 40,000 times since 1984, the year the Clean Water Act was brought in. The companies were fined and forced to clean up their discharges.

South China Sea
Water quality in this area has deteriorated after rapid development. Inshore waters, particularly harbors, bays and estuaries, are discolored. Oil slicks are a common sight. In Hong Kong, breast milk has high levels of DDT and dieldrin. The pesticides are thought to come from the mainly seafood diet.

◁ This penguin is the victim of an oil spill. Its plumage is coated with crude oil.

▽ This map shows how the worst ocean pollution is found mainly on the continental shelves, concentrated around major cities with their huge industrial complexes.

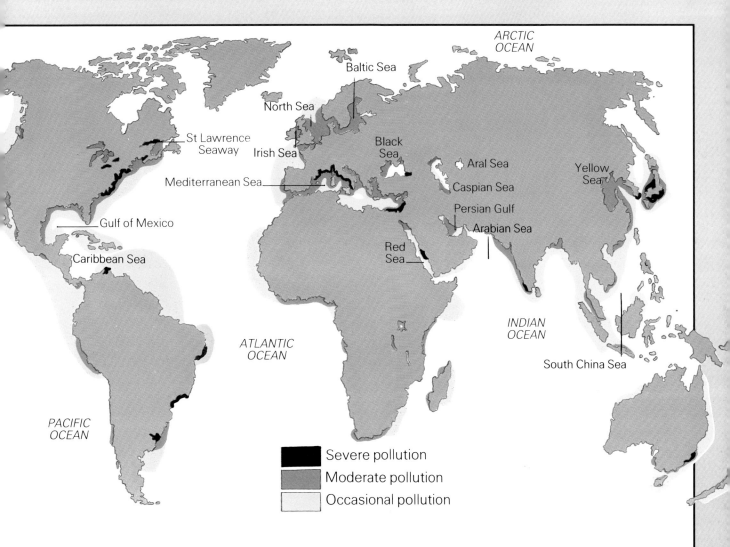

ARCTIC OCEAN

Baltic Sea

North Sea

St Lawrence Seaway

Irish Sea

Black Sea

Aral Sea

Caspian Sea

Yellow Sea

Mediterranean Sea

Persian Gulf

Arabian Sea

Gulf of Mexico

Red Sea

Caribbean Sea

ATLANTIC OCEAN

INDIAN OCEAN

South China Sea

PACIFIC OCEAN

■ Severe pollution
▨ Moderate pollution
☐ Occasional pollution

South Pacific
A British researcher visiting the remote Ducie Atoll in the South Pacific (290 mi from the nearest inhabited island and 3,000 mi from the nearest continent) surveyed a 1½ mi stretch of beach. There he discovered 953 items of garbage. His find included toy soldiers and tanks, a doll's head, 179 buoys, 14 crates, 171 bottles, 268 pieces of plastic, 6 fluorescent tubes, 7 aerosol cans and an asthma inhaler, among other things.

Tasman and Coral seas
The bodies of dead dolphins and whales, washed up on Australia's east coast between 1987 and 1991, contained high levels of pesticides and heavy metals. Most of the corpses were toothed whales and dolphins, indicating that pollutants have contaminated the entire food chain in that part of the world. Two baby whales that had died at birth contained high levels of pollutants that they must have acquired while in the womb.

United States
After a scare in 1988, when medical waste such as hypodermic needles was found along the tideline of beaches near New York, authorities began to take floating garbage seriously. In the summer of 1990, US Army Corps of Engineers deployed boats around New York to pick up 543 tons of garbage. Prisoners cleared the beaches of 3,000 tons, including household, industrial and medical waste.

Index

Photographic Credits:
Cover: Topham; pages 4-5, 7, 14 (top), 17 (top) and 27: Bruce Coleman; pages 8, 10-11, 12, 13 (both), 18, 19 (both), 22 (both), 23, 24, 25 (bottom) and 30: Planet Earth; pages 9, 16-17: Frank Spooner Pictures; page 15 (all): Kieran Mulvaney; page 20 (bottom): Panos Pictures: pages 21 (top), 28 and 29: Greenpeace; page 25 (top): Oxford Scientific Films; page 26: Robert Harding.